THE SHIFT
Poetry for a New Perspective

MELODY GODFRED
The Self Love Philosopher

Illustrated by Leanne Aranador

Andrews McMeel
PUBLISHING®

Andrews McMeel Publishing
a division of Andrews McMeel Universal
1130 Walnut Street, Kansas City, Missouri 64106

www.andrewsmcmeel.com

22 23 24 25 26 VEP 10 9 8 7 6 5 4 3 2 1

ISBN: 978-1-5248-7124-6

Library of Congress Control Number: 2022938601

Editor: Patty Rice
Art Director/Designer: Julie Barnes
Production Editor: Thea Voutiritsas
Production Manager: Shona Burns

ATTENTION: SCHOOLS AND BUSINESSES
Andrews McMeel books are available at quantity discounts with
bulk purchase for educational, business, or sales promotional use.
For information, please e-mail the Andrews McMeel Publishing
Special Sales Department: specialsales@amuniversal.com.

DEDICATION

For my parents, who risked everything
so I could be me.

INTRODUCTION

By January of 2021, I was already deeply entrenched in the inconceivable changes the pandemic had thrust upon us. But it wasn't until the dawning of the new year that I realized something: while the world had changed, so had I. I had shifted. Everything superficial, extraneous, and ego-driven in my life had fallen away. What was left? Only what actually mattered to me. From the isolation and limitations of the pandemic, I was gifted with something I had always wished for: clarity.

So began my work on this book, *The Shift: Poetry for a New Perspective*. Seventy-five pairs of poems that reflect this unique time in all our lives, and reframe how we think and feel about ourselves, our relationships, our world. The left side of every spread conveys the old way; the right side illuminates the new. My hope is that these poems, and their accompanying artwork, either honor a shift you've already experienced or serve as a catalyst for a shift that you need to make.

A note about the cover. I chose monarch butterflies to symbolize the transformation at the heart of *The Shift*. When I've reached critical moments in my life, monarchs have emerged to guide me. After showing this cover to my mother-in-law, an avid gardener, she shared this affirming news with me: while monarch butterflies nearly went extinct in 2020 (under 2,000 spotted in California, a decrease of 99 percent from prior years), during its 2021 migration, the western monarch butterfly population exploded back up to 100,000. A good sign that we, too, are on our road to redemption.

The world has changed. Thankfully, so have we. Welcome to *The Shift*.

Disappointment buried in the hips
Shame dug into shoulders
Sadness woven along bones
This body a graveyard of unfelt feelings
All interred without ceremony
Ghosts carried in limbs
Getting heavier every day.

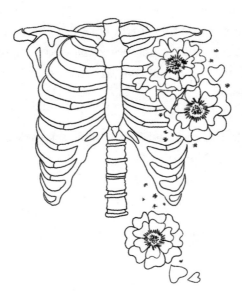

THE SHIFT

I pulled back the earth and
Gently laid down my guilt, fear, and trauma
I watered them with my acceptance and
Watched as they transformed
Once seeds of self doubt
Now a field of self love.

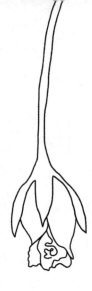

Fear is:
Holding your breath.

Trust is:
Letting go of a lung full of air and
Knowing it will come back to you.
Please breathe.

The clock struck thirteen and
The cities stopped
Shelves swiped clean
Doors shuttered
Roads emptied
Lights out
The end of the world
As we know it.

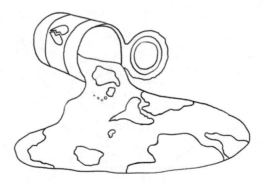

When you need a reminder
That paradise is planted
Not purchased
The garden is available
The sound of birds
So strong
We forgot the hum
Of traffic ever existed.

I sunk down onto the floor
Dropped lower and swam among
The fish of darkness
Is this low enough?
Am I small enough?
Now will you finally catch me?

Head adorned with stars
Body wrapped in clouds
My heart a universe
Open to being explored
As long as you're willing
To reach my orbit.

We climb the hill called more
Because to stop would mean we're less
And settling for enough would mean
We are nothing
So we push a little harder
Spin another plate, and then another
Run on the wheel, faster and faster
Until what's left of us is an empty blur.

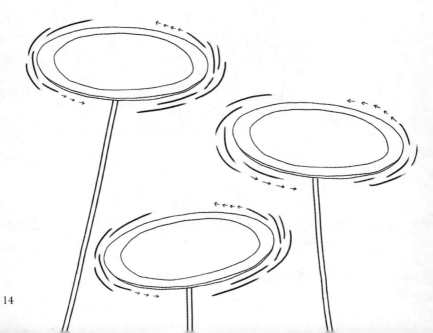

You are the conductor
To pause is your power
Feel the magnitude of a rest
A symphony brewing in silent spaces.

Settle for your
Short-term security or...

...Nurture your
Long-term vision.

I post the squares
That together form
This perfect life
The right words
With the right guise
At the right time
Make you believe
Life in this box
Is oh so nice.

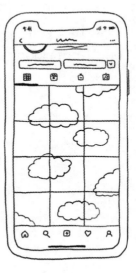

I failed! Perfectly!
I left my zone!
I took a risk!
I danced among my dreams
Instead of standing
In my limitations!

It's selfish to rest
When breakfast must be made
When lunch must be packed
When dinner must be planned
It's selfish to pause
When emails must be checked
When orders must be placed
When bills must be paid
It's selfish, your love
But only when it's for yourself.

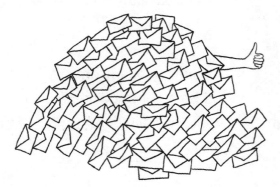

When you finally love yourself
The tests will soon follow
The past will dangle itself before you
Beckoning you like a warm bed
But you weren't born to sleep
You were born to rise.

What I want from you
Is all the things
Fidelity, love
Sex, security
Abundance
Adventure
Every perfect promise
Ever made and more.

The things you offer
I receive with love

The things you withhold
I explore with curiosity

The things I need
I express with clarity

The things we share
I honor with integrity.

The whoosh of would
The slap of should
The kick of could
They leave me
On my knees.

I stand here
Alive in this moment
That in itself
Is enough
That in itself
Is everything.

I jump forward
From one dot to the next
Desperate to understand
The picture that is forming
To ensure the ends will
Justify the means
It will all make sense
As long as I keep
Dragging this line
Forward.

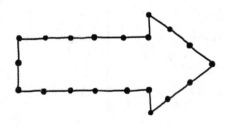

I tell my daughters
"Plans are not promises.
They are allowed to change."
I tell myself, too.

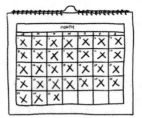

The future:
Fearfully planned.

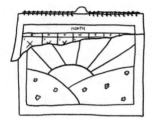

The future:
Joyfully unknown.

Fear submerges us
In a sea of but how?
But when?
Eyes too salted to see
The islands of possibility
Just beyond the crashing waves
The beckoning shore
So close as we slip below.

Love's winds deliver
Unfathomed blessings
They land on our skin
Kisses from a sacred place
We receive them
With trust, with awe
Without needing to
Know a thing more
About why they arrived.

We bought extra supplies
Then we bought some more
We filled the cupboards, the closets
The space between spaces
We bought so much that
We didn't have space for our anxiety
We lied to ourselves —
Anxiety always makes space for itself.

We never ran out
Of what we needed most
Of love
Of love
Of love.

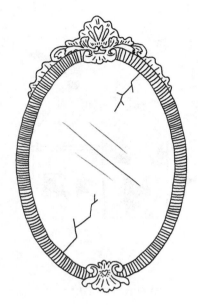

I am envious of her self regard
The space she holds sacred for herself
The time she doesn't have to negotiate for
The identity that is so clear
The woman I once was that lives on in her
I am envious of her self regard
I am envious of her — self.

I slip off the mother
I cast aside the wife
I put away the worker
I relinquish the good friend
The daughter, the savior
I breathe out, I slow down
Right now, all I am, is here, for me.

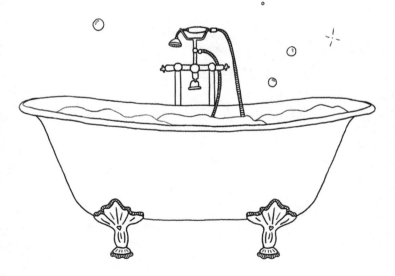

Scrambling toward chaos
Chasing after sirens
Fixing emotional potholes
In every soul I meet
Their resulting wholeness
Now the barometer of mine.

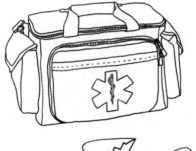

THE SHIFT

Once I realized
My time is mine for me
My energy is mine for me
My healing is mine for me
My love is mine for me
My joy is mine for me
The ones with whole souls
Found their way to me.

Wait in pain or...

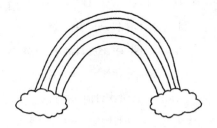

...Anticipate with pleasure.

In a world that rules a woman's body
We are expected to spin in retrograde:
The instant we deliver life
We must erase the proof
Reverse the scale
Smooth the lines
Conceal the grays, and
Stand up straight despite
The children on our hips and
The weight of their futures
On our backs.

They call them stretch marks
Because it's true — I stretched
Beyond my body
Beyond my mind
Beyond my identity
Beyond my comfort
Beyond my limits
Beyond my wildest dreams.

Is unconditional love
Saying yes even when
The truth is no?
An ever-expanding
space we occupy forever
Because we once
Promised we would?

This love has edges
They let us know when
We've strayed too far
From ourselves
From each other
From home.

My worth used to live
In my closet, in my car
In the jewel box by my bed
In the interest of strangers
In the approval of teachers
In the acceptance of girls who
Never questioned their worth
Not once.

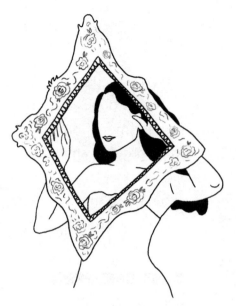

I went to the museum
Stood in front of the
Most coveted piece
And realized I, too
Am a one-of-a-kind
Work of art.

Write the list
Get it done
Ask for more and
Don't forget to smile
How lucky you are
To have so much
To take care of.

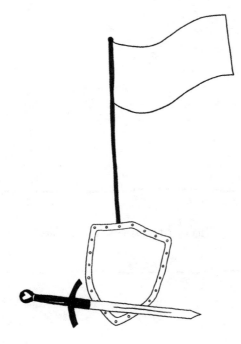

Some days you will feel victorious
Some days you will feel defeated
Either way, you are still a warrior.

The confinement of routine.

The liberation of ritual.

I held the trial
I was the judge, and the jury
The prosecutor, and the defense
Not a single witness, because
I carried out my crimes in solitude
I was the perpetrator, I was the victim
I did it to myself, like I always do.

I carry with me now
A chorus
Mercy, Grace, and Faith
Always singing for me:
"You did your best
You did your best
You did your best."
Their loving refrain.

When your ego screams:
"Be better!"

Listen to your soul who whispers:
"Grow."

Eyes drunk on potential
The true shape of you
Blurred by the holy light
Of my most hopeful love

Mouth too busy
Coating your words
With forgiveness
To actually hear them

You cast off my veil
Begging to be seen
For what you were
And weren't

You never hid from me
I hid you from myself.

The best of us
The worst of us
Our love is bathed in truth
We survive its currents
Not on a lifeboat of hope
But in a vessel of trust.

I see what is meant to be seen
I follow the rules
I stay within the lines
I submit to the routine
I keep myself safe
I make sure it all makes sense
I call it a life.

I hear honey
I taste red
I smell softness
I see melodies
I touch childhood memories
That remind me what
It means to be alive.

We put on a brave face
When we're brave and
Also when we're not
Because that is what
Brave people do.

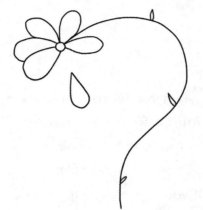

When the flower blooms
She blooms
When the flower wilts
She wilts
There is no shame
In her journey.

When you hit rock bottom
And things get even worse
You have two choices:
Suffer the despair
Of your downward spiral, or...

...Celebrate the joy
Of your continued resilience.
Your choice.

It is broken.

It is born.

In this house, we are protected
We know what tomorrow brings
We recognize it as yesterday
Disguised in a coat of falling leaves
Or sticky with sweat and salt and sand
We will recognize it nonetheless
It's exactly what we expected
It's exactly what will let us down.

Let's swim together
To the edge of our comfort zone
Toes dangling over the future
Eyes beaming, hearts bursting
One, two, three...
Jump.

I'll carry your pain
To prove that I am strong
I'll solve your problems
To prove that I am smart
I'll forgive your failures
To prove that I am loving
Now do we believe in me?

My mom said that she
Regrets throwing away
My childhood trophies
So I reminded her:
"I am the prize."

Hide the proof
Ignore the pain
Rush here and there
Forgo the rest
It's business as usual
Even though what we do
Is bleed.

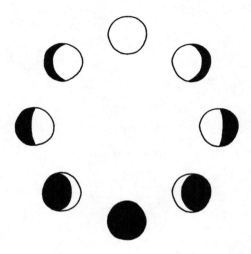

This steady cycle a reminder
That our bodies are precious
That we deserve care and rest
That even when all seems lost
We can and will begin again.

Forcing it
May get you
What you want
But...

...Allowing it
Will get you
What you need.

The hallway dark, and endless
A parade of doors with polished knobs
I knocked, I waited, I knocked again
I twisted each gently, then with force
Only to feel the unmistakable resistance
Of a lock not meant to be freed.

The moment
I stopped
Trying to open
Every door
The right doors
Started to open
With ease
With joy
Without a lock
In sight.

Who am I without my needs?
I am nothing but sand at the shore
Waiting for your tides to push me away
Waiting for you to pull me back.

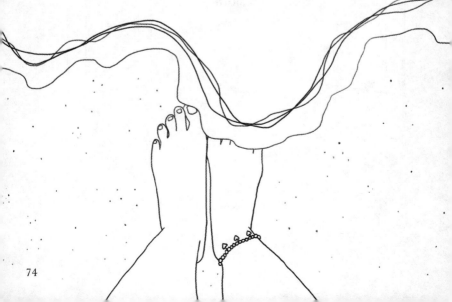

When I protect
The lines between us
It's not to keep us apart
It's to allow the
True versions of us
To stay together.

I wear self sacrifice
Like a dress
She conceals my needs
As I twirl and twirl
To avoid the truth
Of stillness.

When I stopped
Treading water
Instead of sinking
I remembered
I can swim.

Let's tuck it away
No need to talk
Not tonight, we agree
I put my pain in the cool spot
In the corner of our bed
Now warming with
Unspoken anger
Trapped in our sheets
Worse than any affair
We cheat each other here
Right here.

Our love is a confessional
Where all truth is welcome
We come together uncertain
We leave each other absolved.

A quilt of boredom
Drowns my soul to sleep
I try to find myself in its folds
But only end up
Reinforcing my patterns
Habit by habit
Stitch by stitch.

Curiosity is a hummingbird
Singing in my ear
I feel her vibrations
As I follow her wings
Iridescent plumes
Of rainbow light
Guiding me to
The nectar of life
Guiding me
Home
To me.

No time for eye contact
No time for smiles
No time for small talk
No time for kindness
No hard feelings, there's
Just no time.

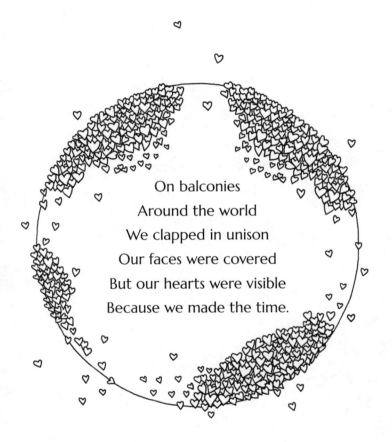

On balconies
Around the world
We clapped in unison
Our faces were covered
But our hearts were visible
Because we made the time.

If I work hard enough
I will finally get to
Where I'm going.

If I rest gently enough
I will finally be present
Where I am.

Nothing is born of resistance.

Everything is born of surrender.

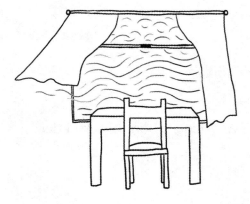

I can see it
The perfect room
The room where I will write
Light abounds and there's a soft breeze
I'm comfortable and focused
The words pour out of me.

Anywhere I am
The words are, too
I am light and breezy
Comfortable and focused
The words pour out of me.

I have two homes
One in the past
Where I live with my regrets
One in the future
Where I live with my fears
I have two homes, but
Where I live, is never here.

This heart is grateful
This mind is grateful
This body is grateful
This soul is grateful
I welcome life in with
Every cell
Every breath
Every waking and
Dreaming thought
I am in constant wonder
In constant awe:
Oh to be alive and well
Here together, now.

$f(x) = x^2$

Aren't you tired?
The infinite calculus
Of mapping out every outcome
Must be exhausting.

$\int f(x)\,dx$

$m\frac{d^2 x}{dt^2} = -kx$

THE SHIFT

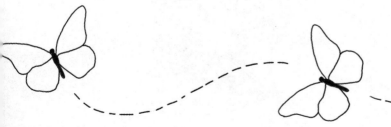

Like the monarch butterfly
I need no clock
To tell me when it is time to go
No map to show me where to land
Like the monarch
I shift when migration beckons
And emerge where the warm sun glows.

Constantly being in control
Doesn't just tame your environment
It also cages you
Bars made of unmet expectations
The floor cold with banality
Wouldn't you rather be free?

THE SHIFT

The pain of shedding
This familiar skin
Vibrates throughout me
But inch by inch
I carry myself forward
Toward my deepest desires
Beyond my perfect control
Into the naked freedom
Of a new beginning.

"I deserve closure!"
— Your ego

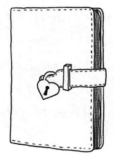

"I desire peace."
— Your soul

I am here
And you are here
And this ledge
Is only big enough
For one of us to be right.

I broke through
My ego's armor
And discovered that
Behind my anger
Was my fear
Beyond my
Need to be right
Was my birthright
To feel peace
And between us was
An ocean of love
Patiently waiting
For us to set sail.

I dug this tunnel
Where only I can see
I built this chamber
Where only I can hear
I would invite you in but
There's only room for one.

When you speak to others
Leave room for the possibility
That you are wrong
The same is true for
When you speak to yourself.

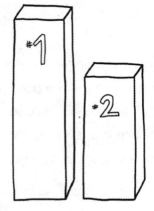

Praise says,
"I see what you've done
And I approve of you."

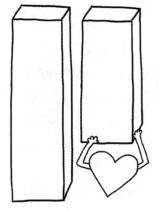

Empathy says,
"I see who you are
And I stand with you."

Paint peeling
Lights flickering
Internet lagging
Drywall crumbling
Hinges sagging
Clutter mounting
Not a single place
For these all-seeing
Eyes to rest.

A home
Filled with books
Children, laughter
And life
Exactly what
We wished for
And more.

Generational trauma
Weighs us down.

Generational healing
Sets us free.

When fight or flight
Is coded in your DNA
There is no resting heartbeat
Every moment is a threat
Every opportunity is a risk
Every place is a danger zone
Every person is an adversary
Every action is an error
Every thought is a dagger
And chaos is as comfortable
As this life will ever get.

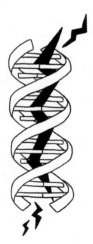

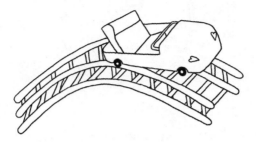

And who knew it was possible
To anticipate the rides up
Instead of the free.falls
To meet each moment not with dread
But with hope and joy and trust
So much struggle endured
Before I learned to relax, to rest
To float instead of sink.

Hold on, one more month
By May, it will be okay
Hold on, one more week
By August, it will be okay
Hold on, one more day
By December, it will be okay
Hold on, one more hour
One more minute
Just hold on.

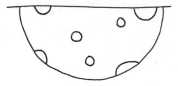

Rise by the sun
Retire by the moon
And in between
Make a life worth living.

Your words closed
Around my throat
Leaving me stuck between
Silence and a scream
Suspended in the terror
Of knowing I'm ruined
Either way.

Your words are gliding
In the space between us
I observe them
Without attachment
And wonder if
I'll offer any of them
A nest.

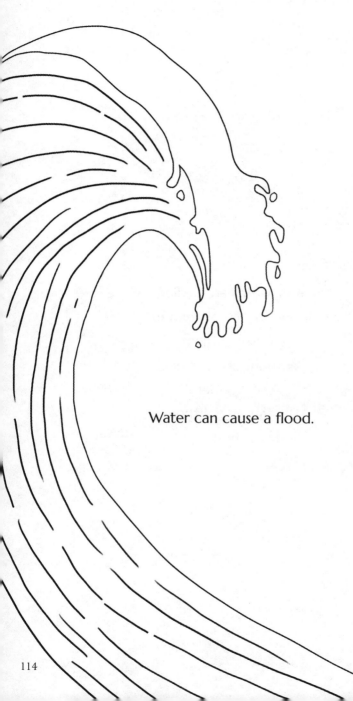

Water can cause a flood.

Water can put out a fire.

Your thoughts
They are the water.

Choose them wisely.

Everything I am, is yours.
Everything I am not, is mine.

I crave partnership that claims
Not only my fullness
But my vast emptiness
The uncertain future
The regrettable past
I want you to beg for all of it.

Look, up in the sky!
It's a bird!
It's a plane!
It is SUPERWOMAN
She does it all and
Has it all, all at once
All by herself
How does she do it?
She does it alone.

When help is offered
Please take it
Without condition
Without comparison
Without expectation
Without disappointment
Without clinging
To the burden
It was meant to alleviate.

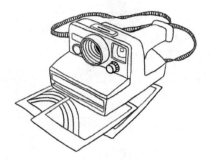

We're so busy
Capturing the moment
We forgo being
Captured by the moment.

THE SHIFT

The rain stopped
The sun shone
The clouds melted
The air glittered
I looked up and my
Rainbow was waiting
Exactly where I gazed
For just a moment, just for me
No proof she happened
Other than her smiling arc
Glimmering in my mind, forever.

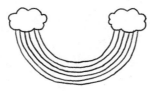

If I am strong enough
I will figure out the code
I will perfectly arrange
All the pieces
I will.

If I am strong enough
Nothing will slip
Nothing will break
Don't get too close
I'm holding
So many pieces.

If I let go
What happens?
Will it be okay?
Am I okay?
I am.

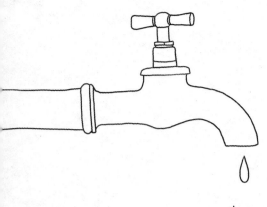

The drip drop of grief
Leaking into this life
Keeps me up at night
My resilience
Simply the stain
My grief left behind.

Joy is always
Ready to be watered
She wants to
Grow, grow, grow.

When safety demands solitude
How can we not feel alone?
When healing requires hibernation
How can we not feel asleep?
When a polarized present
Threatens a shared future
How can we not feel divided?
When survival calls for endurance
Of endless loss upon loss
How can we not feel like
What was normal
Is no longer?

THE SHIFT

Today I reached for the sky with my eyes
I put my arms up and pulled forward
The sun and moon's shared promise:
Of life continuing
Of dreams manifesting
Of an awakening
And so I released the fearful breath
I've been holding now for years
The hibernation over
As a new era begins.

Scroll away my pain
Swipe away my fear
Click away my anxiety
Stream away my sadness
This is my me time
I deserve this, I tell myself.

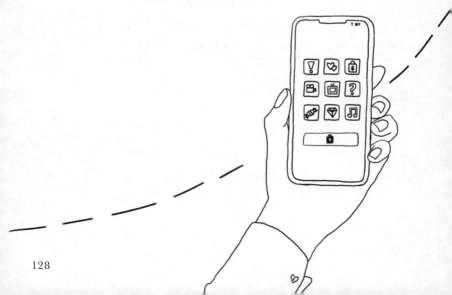

Will you live it?
This life that is yours?
Or will you let distraction
Lay claim to your treasure?

Every friend
I've ever made
Must come along
Forevermore
We pile into one life
Through every stage
We're stuck together
It isn't comfortable
But this is what
True friends do
Isn't it?

I gifted myself
Your absence
And only then
Did I realize
Just how heavy
A shared history
Can be.

I lay myself out
Like a dining table
A feast of love
Reserved for one
My fullness
Yours for the taking
Aloof as ever
You take it all
All without taking
A single bite.

THE SHIFT

When we learn
To love ourselves
We set the table
For others to join us
Not everyone can, or will
But whether they come, or go
We will never be hungry
Or lonely again.

Forward forward
Faster faster
Hurry!
Father Time insists
And yet
I'm never fully awake
Until I'm certain
I'll be fifteen minutes late
To where I need to be.

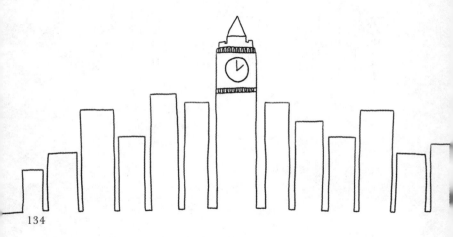

THE SHIFT

Mother, mother
I hear you loud and clear
Moonlight over blue light
Wind over recycled air
Dirt over bleach
Leaves over keys
To be of the earth
Not simply on the earth
To remember my nature
Is nature
I'm on my way.

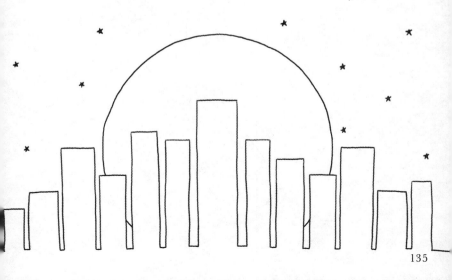

MELODY GODFRED

I tucked them away, all my bests
The champagne, the jewels
The dress — you know the one
I saved them for a special occasion
Today not reason enough to celebrate
Maybe tomorrow, maybe?

Can you feel it?
The sun on your skin?
The air in your lungs?
The momentum of this moment?
If being alive isn't enough
Tell me, what is?

Everyone
Has an opinion, but...

...Only you
Have your intuition.
Trust yourself.

What kind of mother
Leaves her child
To check emails
To write messages
To stare at a screen
Alone in a distant room
What kind of mother?

You help women
Become more powerful
Just by being
Who they are.

All the time I spent
Surrounded by toxic people
I thought I was healing them
When all the while
They were making me sick.

My wounds
Only started to heal
When I realized
I, too, am a patient
Worthy of my care
Deserving of my time
In need of my attention.

I plant all the seeds
And I water them
Even when I thirst
For who am I
If my branches are bare?
What am I worth
Without shiny fruit to offer?

THE SHIFT

Judge not my branches
Instead ask me of my roots
How deep do they run
What weight do they hold
As they humbly grow in hidden spaces
To deliver tomorrow's promise?

Ask not of my fruit
But rather of my fruition
A future cultivated not by doing more
But by nurturing less
Each bough I prune
A commitment to my vitality.

Seek not my flowers
Though they're heavy with dew
And smell of jasmine in the night
Find the rings of my bark
And when you count them
Remember who I've been
And how I got here.

The wear is starting to show
In our faces, our voices, our eyes
I see it in them, my children
Past the point of resistance
They are resigned
The great wait
They wear it bravely
But it's heavy
And they are tired
I am tired, too.

And just when it became
Too heavy to carry
Too hard to climb
Too thick to breathe
Too late to change
I felt something new:
I am
Reset
Renewed
Revived
Reclaimed.

You can't
Have it all, but...

...You can have
What you have.
Will you have it?

I started to grow weary
Thinking about
Six trips to the hospital
In two years
The same outfit
Every time
The duffle bag
Packed with essentials
Like granola bars and fear
Will we get better
Like the doctors hope?

But then I shifted and
The weariness lifted
As soon as instead
Of the trips to the hospital
I remembered the trips home.

A year ago
We reached
Our limits.

A year from now
We will realize
We are limitless.

How do I explain
The others that I am?
Woman, immigrant
The girl who fled
Before she could walk?
The thinker, the feeler
The worker, the creative?
Which language
Will I speak today?
Which identity will I claim?
What happens to my story
If even I don't know
How to tell it?

THE SHIFT

When I was born in Iran
And forced to flee
At three months old
My soul was most certainly
A burning shade of red.
The trauma of survival will do that.

When I was seven In Los Angeles
And learned to play the piano and sing
My soul turned bluer with every note.
So soft and safe and fluid and free.

When my teenage years
Caused my heart to grow
Faster than my body
And I was falling in love
Before I was ready
My soul darkened into a deep purple
As it ached and ached and ached.

When I left my adolescence and
Realized that my essence was still intact
My soul turned green with possibility
As it found my cracks and filled them.

When I discovered self love
My soul became a kaleidoscope
As I finally embraced every woman
I have been, and ever will be.
I am all the others.
I am ME.

Also by Melody Godfred

Self Love Poetry

The ABCs of Self Love

ACKNOWLEDGMENTS

This book wouldn't be possible without the partnership of Leanne Aranador, my longtime illustrator and dear friend. Leanne not only beautifully illustrated all the artwork in *The Shift*, she also conceptualized much of it as well. Leanne would read each poem and then capture its most profound meaning through her art. Thank you, Leanne. I love you.

I also have tremendous gratitude and love for my immediate family. To Aaron, Stella, Violet, Teddy, Yahya, Jackie, Jonny, Danny, Chelsie, and Lupe: thank you for being my joy and comfort throughout the pandemic. You made a suddenly very small life an incredibly fulfilling one.

A big thank you to everyone at my publishing house, Andrews McMeel, for championing my work, especially my editor Patty Rice, who discovered me when I was self-publishing and made my lifelong dream of being a published author come true. Thank you to my agent Erin Hosier, who encouraged me to write the proposal for this book mere months after I finished *Self Love Poetry*, and has been by my side ever since. A special thank you to Amy Makkabi, who was a daily sounding board and source of inspiration for the poems in *The Shift*.

I am also profoundly thankful to all my friends, family, and readers, who consistently cheer for me and empower me to show up as my most authentic self, a writer. Thank you for reading early drafts, offering feedback, ordering my books on launch day, writing reviews, and generously sharing me and my books with your communities. I couldn't do this without you.

ABOUT THE AUTHOR

Melody Godfred is the Self Love Philosopher. As a poet, author, and speaker, she is devoted to empowering people to love themselves and transform their lives. She is the creator of the Self Love Pinky Ring™ and author of *Self Love Poetry: For Thinkers & Feelers* and *The ABCs of Self Love: A Simple Guide to Loving Yourself, Reclaiming Your Worth, and Changing Your Life*. Her poetry has been featured on *Oprah Daily*, *TODAY with Hoda & Jenna*, and *Woman's Day*, among others, for its wisdom and ability to deeply resonate and uplift.

Melody lives in Los Angeles with the loves of her life, Aaron, Stella, Violet, and Teddy. Learn more at melodygodfred.com and connect with her @melodygodfred.